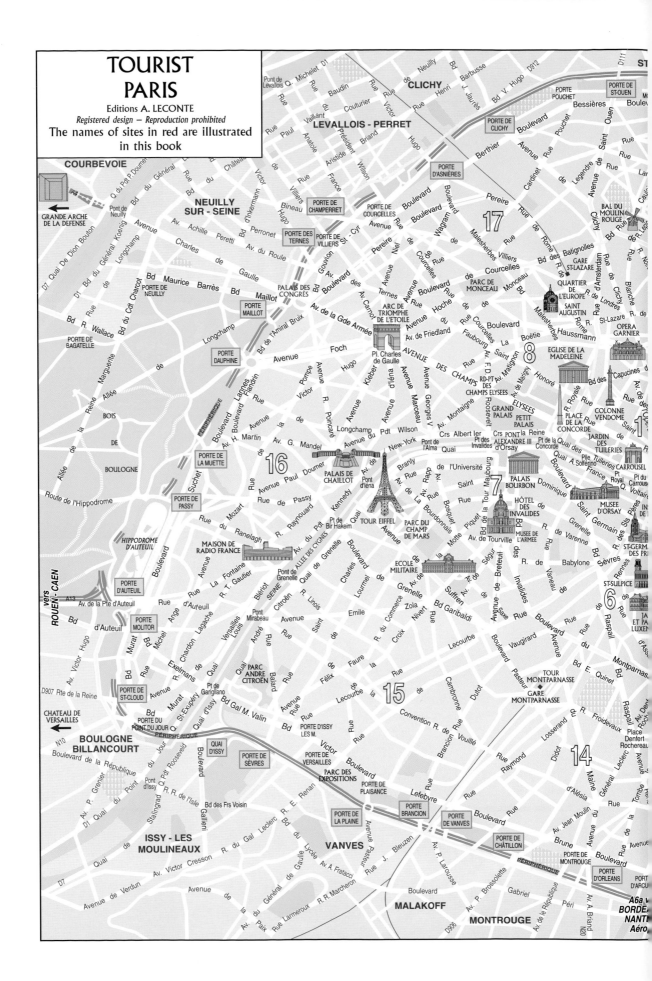

TOURIST PARIS

Editions A. LECONTE

Registered design – Reproduction prohibited

The names of sites in red are illustrated
in this book

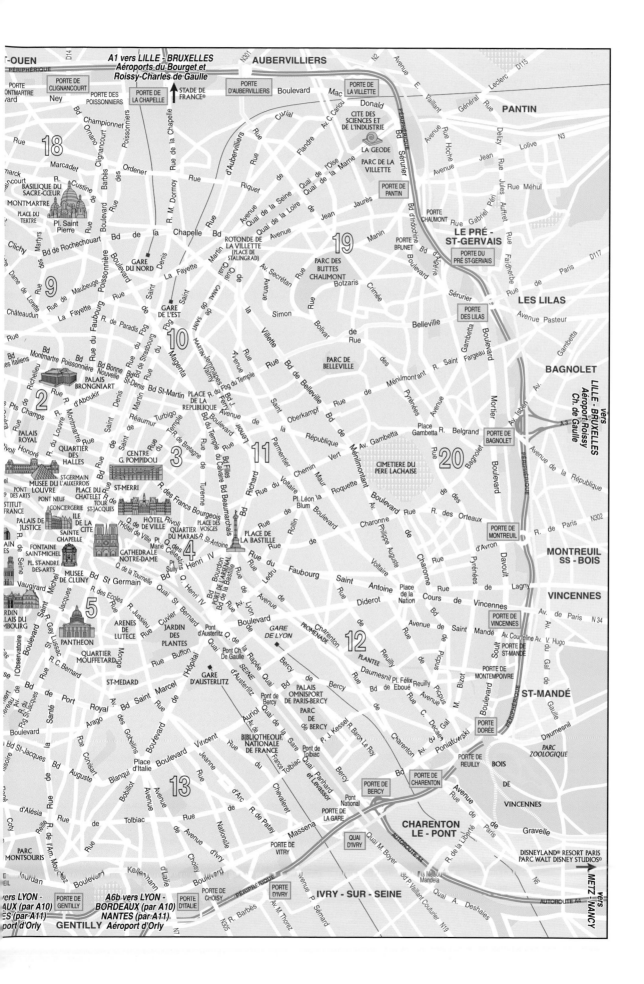

FROM LUTETIA TO TODAY

Paris, City of Light, Paris, the most beautiful city in the world... What superlatives have not been used to describe our capital! We Parisians are also grateful to all the tourists, travellers and visitors who appreciate and admire our beautiful city. We wanted this book to reflect our own affection for Paris, hoping that through these pages the reader will come to share our feelings.

Originally a fishing village of the Parisii tribe on the largest island on the Seine, Lutetia, which rebelled against Caesar (52 BC), was attacked by Labienus who travelled down the Seine to the site of Saint-Germain l'Auxerrois, on the right bank. Camulogène the Gaul was camped on the left bank on the site of Saint-Germain-des-Prés. A stratagem gave victory to the Romans.

Under the first emperors, Lutetia was a pleasant provincial city. The Ile de la Cité devoted its temples to the gods and an imperial palace to power. The city grew up on the left bank, along the road to Orléans. Under Tiberius a new town covered the hill of Sainte-Geneviève. The centre of this district is now the Luxembourg Gardens. The arenas were on the other side of the hill, outside the walls.

From 258 the Barbarians laid waste to Lutetia. The inhabitants shut themselves into the hastily fortified Ile de la Cité. After a further invasion in 355, the Emperor Constans sent his brother-in-law Julian to be governor of northern Gaul. He settled in Lutetia, in the Cité, where his legionnaires proclaimed him an emperor in 360. One century later the Huns arrived at the walls of Lutetia. St Geneviève persuaded the inhabitants not to flee and saved the Cité.

The Merovingians built a capital, but the palace and wooden walls of these Franks vanished with their dynasty. The Carolingians moved their capitals to the east of the empire. Lutetia, now known as Paris, still in the Cité, in 885 barred the Seine to the Danes who wished to ravage the towns upstream. The defence of the Cité was commanded by Eudes, count of France. The Danes retreated and he received the title of king. He was the first Capetian, and this was the start of the fortune of Paris which was then to develop along both banks around the monasteries.

In 1183 Philippe Auguste had two great halls built; in 1186 the town was paved; in 1190 the city wall on the right bank was constructed and in 1209 that on the left bank. Building took place both inside and outside the walls and the King protected his rampart over the Seine with the huge dungeon of the Louvre...

Charles V (1364-1380) built a second enclosure on the right bank surrounding the Hôtel St-Paul, the king's new residence; the Célestins, Maison du Temple; Saint-Martin-des-Champs; Saint-Nicolas-des-Champs; Rue Montorgueil; Rue Montmartre. The wall connected the Seine and the Louvre, following a path corresponding to Rue d'Aboukir, Place des Victoires and the Palais Royal. This wall was fortified to the east by a fortress guarding the Vincennes road.

In the 16th and early 17th centuries, expansion of the city continued towards the west, so much so that Louis XIII extended the Paris of Charles V with a wall which encircled it from Porte Saint-Denis to the borders of the Tuileries.

Louis XIV, affected by the Frondes which humiliated him, installed his government at Versailles. Nonetheless he embellished his capital, transformed the Louvre, built the Hôtel des Invalides, Salpêtrière and the Observatoire, surrounding the town with a ring of triumphal gates and creating the squares of Victoires and Vendôme...

The Ile de la Cité, cradle of the capital: Notre Dame Cathedral represents zero kilometres, the hub of all the major routes radiating from Paris.

To Louis XV we owe the Concorde, the Ecole Militaire, the Hôtel de la Monnaie and the Palais de Justice, but it was in the reign of Louis XVI that Paris was completely transformed with the implementation of 3 measures: the width of new roads was set at 9.75 m, the construction of an enclosure in 1784, called 'Fermiers Généraux', which took the limits of Paris to the outer boulevards and the demolition of all the houses built on the bridges of Paris. Long views of the Seine appeared, much as we see it today.

Napoleon I had a plan to make Paris "the most beautiful city possible". For him, architecture and town planning went hand in hand. He created not only bridges, embankments, market halls, abattoirs, the Arc de Triomphe de l'Etoile, the great highways and churches but also a water supply system, diverting the waters of the Ourcq to supply the city and constructing the Villette basin, aqueducts and numerous public fountains.

The outstanding development of the Restoration period was the formation of the aristocratic quarter of Faubourg Saint-Germain.

The last major changes, before 20th century Paris, were made under Napoleon III, with Baron Haussmann's considerable works, together with the anarchic industrialisation of the suburbs and faubourgs. Then there was the World Fair of 1889 and the appearance of an initially controversial, but later celebrated, monument, the Eiffel Tower... But Paris never ceases to change...

While it is true that "Paris will always be Paris", over the centuries the capital has also known how to dress itself up with some magnificent sites where kings and the men in high places found peace and quiet away from the noise and bustle of the big city. Thus we have Versailles, where the shadow of the Sun King still reigns...

... And nearby on a new and enchanting site, we have the DISNEYLAND® RESORT PARIS and WALT DISNEY STUDIOS© theme parks.

Enjoy your visit!

The arenas of Lutetia (first century AD), whose shape and layout were designed to permit both theatrical performances and circus games in ancient times.

Paris past and present: in the Cour Napoléon, architect Ieoh Ming Pei's pyramid, with buildings constructed by Percier and Fontaine under the First Empire, then by Visconti and Lefuel under the Second Empire.

Notre Dame Cathedral, begun in 1163 on the orders of Bishop Maurice de Sully, was completed in 1330. The ravages of time and the Revolution made restoration necessary. This was carried out between 1841 and 1864 by Viollet-le-Duc, who in particular rebuilt the spire which reaches a height of 90m.

Notre Dame Cathedral, from the banks of the Seine (19th century engraving).

◀ In the Ile de la Cité: the Square Jean XXIII and Notre Dame Cathedral, the Police headquarters, the Commercial court, the Palais de Justice and the Sainte-Chapelle.

The Seine and its bridges (bottom to top, left to right): Pont de l'Archevêché, Pont Saint-Louis, Pont-au-Double, Pont d'Arcole, Petit-Pont, Pont Notre-Dame, Pont Saint-Michel, Pont-au-Change, Pont Neuf, Pont des Arts.

On the right bank: the Théâtre de la Ville and the Théâtre du Châtelet, the Louvre Palace and the Tuileries gardens.

"Charlemagne and his Liegemen" in the style of Formigé. The Emperor, on horseback, is led by Olivier and Roland. The latter's sword, Durandal, is an exact copy of the original, which is still kept in Madrid.

NOTRE DAME CATHEDRAL

The Parvis of Notre Dame graces the Cathedral whose towers rise 69 m above the ground. The façade is divided into four levels:

1 - the 3 portals, with left to right:
- The north portal, constructed first, in the second decade of the 13th century, in honour of the Virgin Mary.
- The central portal, known as the "Last Judgment", where Christ, having returned to judge the living and the dead, dominates the statues of St Michael and Satan.
- The south portal, known as St Anne's, placed under the sign of the Virgin presenting her child, framed by two thurifer angels behind whom can be seen, on the right, King Louis VII, and on the left, Maurice de Sully.

2 - the Kings' gallery, with a line of statues of the 28 kings of Judah and Israel;

3 - the rose window 9.60 m in diameter, framed by two arched recesses in which stand statutes of Adam on the left and Eve on the right ;

4 - a tracery gallery surmounted by a balustrade, a kingdom of chimeras, ghouls, demons and monsters in addition to the famous gargoyles, themselves dominated by two towers from which you can enjoy a magnificent view of the capital.

Under the square, the largest archaeological crypt in Europe narrates the history of Paris from recently conducted excavations.

◀   The interior of the cathedral extending to a length of 127.50 m for a height of 32.50 m beneath the vaults and capable of holding -with the galleries- about 9000 of the faithful, according to the calculations of Viollet-le-Duc. In the centre of the transept, the podium is surmounted by a bronze altar consecrated in 1989, the work of Jean and Sébastien Touret.

    The stained glass in the north rose window shows, in the centre, the Virgin holding the Holy Child to her bosom, surrounded by sixteen prophets. In the second circle are thirty-two kings and ancestors of Christ and, crowning the whole, thirty-two patriarchs and high priests of Israel.   ▶

    At the back of the Chancel, the high altar and the group of sculptures represents "the vow of Louis XIII": the king, right, and his son Louis XIV on the left, either side of the Pietà group by Nicolas Coustou (1723). A Cross of Glory has recently been added, symbolising the triumph of the Resurrection. ▼

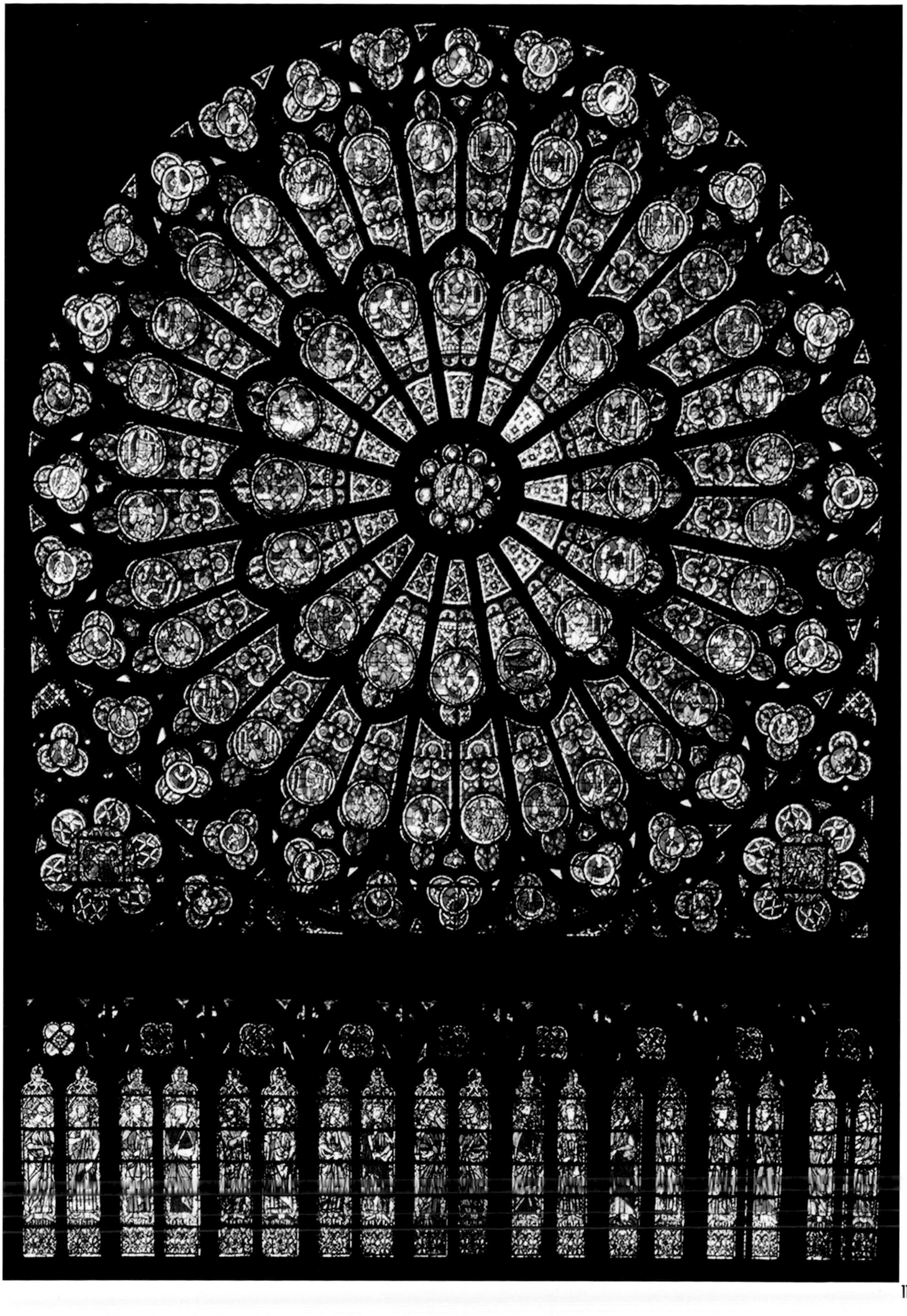

LAW COURTS

The entrance to the Palais de Justice, opening onto Cour de Mai [May Court] which owes its name to the fact that the clerks used to plant a tree here every year at that time. On this site were successively built the residence of the Roman governors of Lutetia, that of the Merovingian kings, then, under the name of Palais de la Cité, that of the kings of France, until 1358. Then the kings deserted it, following riots led by Etienne Marcel, who, forcing the gates of the future Charles V, then dauphin [crown prince], forced him to don a hood in the colours of Paris, and cut the throats of his advisors before his eyes. The place then became the palace of the Parliament, supreme court of the monarchy.

Today the site is divided into four parts: for the Police - the famous Quai d'Orfèvres, for Justice, for La Conciergerie, a place of incarceration from the end of the 14th century until 1914, and for the spiritual world of the Middle Ages, symbolised by la Sainte-Chapelle.

SAINTE-CHAPELLE

La Sainte-Chapelle, a gem of Gothic art, was constructed between 1246 and 1248, on the orders of St Louis, to house the holy relics ceded to the king of France by the Emperor of the East, Baudouin II - Christ's crown of thorns and a fragment of the cross. The building, attributed to Pierre de Montreuil, 36 m long, 17 m wide and 42.50 m high, contains two chapels one above the other. The upper chapel was reserved for the royal family and the great dignitaries of the court, and the lower chapel was for the servants.

The site is equally remarkable for its stained-glass windows which tell the story of the Old Testament, the Passion and the Resurrection of Christ, and the lives of the Virgin Mary, John the Baptist and John the Evangelist.

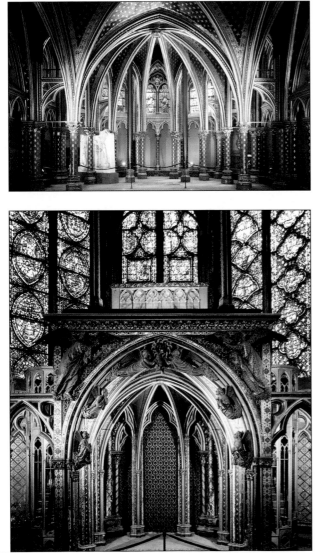

CONCIERGERIE

So called because this part of the Palace was placed under the authority of the "concierge", a high ranking royal official. As you travel downstream a square tower can be seen, known as the "Tour de l'Horloge" [clock tower] which houses the oldest clock in Paris (1370), two twin towers flanking the former entrance -Tour de César and Tour d'Argent, the latter containing the royal treasury - and the Bonbec tower, so called because prisoners were tortured there. Under the Revolution, 4174 prisoners were detained here, including Queen Marie-Antoinette from 2 August to 16 October 1793. Within, of particular interest are: the room known as the Chapelle des Girondins, the Cour des Femmes [Women's courtyard] and the courtyard known as Cour des Douze [Courtyard of the Twelve] where those condemned to death in 1793 and 1794 were assembled in groups of that number.

In the Ile de la Cité, the most famous and oldest bridge in Paris: the Pont Neuf.

The first stone was laid on 31 May 1578 by Henri III. Henri IV inaugurated it on 20 June 1603. Under Louis XIII it acquired a curious reputation:

"You, meeting place of charlatans,
Of rogues and 'passe-volans'
[soldiers in name only who attended parades
to justify excessive army accounts]
Pont Neuf, commonplace theatre
Of sellers of ointments and patches ;
Resting place for tooth pullers,
Secondhand clothes sellers, booksellers, wordsmiths,
Singers of new songs,
Pimps of young maidens
Cutpurses, the foul-mouthed,
Masters of all evil trades..."

(Les filouteries de Pont Neuf)
[The swindles of Pont Neuf]

Dominating the square du Vert-Galant, the equestrian statue of Henri IV, erected in 1818. It replaced its predecessor, destroyed on 14 August 1792, which had been put there in 1614, commissioned by Marie de Médicis.

An example of "Art nouveau" of the early 20th century, La Samaritaine was built between 1926 and 1928 to the plans of the architect Henri Sauvage, commissioned by Ernest Cognacq, nicknamed the "Napoléon du déballage" [the Napoleon of display]. Today it is still one of the capital's largest department stores.

The church of Saint-Germain l'Auxerrois, on the right, constructed in the 12th to 16th centuries and restored in the 19th. The belfry, in the centre, includes a 38-bell campanile, including the bell "Marie", which rang Saint-Bartholomew in the night of 23 to 24 August 1572. On the left is the town hall of the 1st arrondissement (1859).

TOUR SAINT JACQUES

Tour Saint-Jacques - height 52 m - is a remnant of the former church of Saint-Jacques-la-Boucherie (1508-1522) destroyed in 1797, during the Revolution. Its name was associated with the corporation of butchers, animal skinners and tanners, then later with Nicolas Flamel who was one of its main benefactors.

Nearby is Place du Châtelet, which takes its name from the old fortress called Grand Châtelet, a sinister prison which was razed to the ground shortly after the Revolution. The present fountain, known as "du Palmier" occupies the centre of this square. Begun in 1806, the column is decorated with palm leaves between which are inscribed the names of Napoleon Bonaparte's campaigns in Egypt and Italy. A winged statue of Victory, the work of Bosio, tops the column.

PALAIS ROYAL

It was Cardinal Richelieu who had the idea of this palace, in 1629. He entrusted the plans for it to his architect, Jacques Le Mercier, and the gardens to Degots. On his death, he left the house to King Louis XIII, which henceforth became the Palais Royal. Louis XIV inherited it, granted it to his brother Gaston d'Orléans, whose descendants retained it until 1848. In 1786 the Duke of Chartres had 60 pavilions added, the rents for which enabled him to pay his debts. The site became the theatre for various entertainments: "There was nothing there but some booksellers, poets, political activists and wordsmiths, some fashion retailers and lastly ladies of pleasure who came only in the evenings..." (Balzac - Lost Illusions).

Today the area is a haven of tranquillity. The buildings house the Council of State, the Constitutional Council, the Comédie Française and the Ministry of Culture.

The name Carrousel was given to this square in which Louis XIV gave a grand fête in 1662, in honour of Mademoiselle de La Vallière. Between 1806 and 1808, Percier and Fontaine built the present triumphal arch here, an imitation of that of Septimius Severus in Rome, to the glory of Napoleon I's victories in Italy. ▼

LOUVRE

At first a royal château constructed by Philippe Auguste in 1204, transformed by Charles V from 1364 to 1380, it was completely rebuilt between the time of François I and the 19th century. The differing styles of four centuries have thus left their mark.

The new Louvre was built by Percier and Fontaine under the First Empire and by Visconti and Lefuel under the Second. It is here, in the cour Napoléon [Napoleon courtyard], that the Pyramid now stands, work of the architect Ieoh Ming Pei (Public section of the Grand Louvre).

Finally, the old Louvre, with its famous Cour Carrée [Square Courtyard], brings together some remarkable architectural features: Pierre Lescot's façade, Lemercier's 'pavillon de l'Horloge' [the Clock Pavilion] and the colonnade on the east façade by Claude Perrault.

This mecca of the arts, today houses one of the largest museum collections in the world.

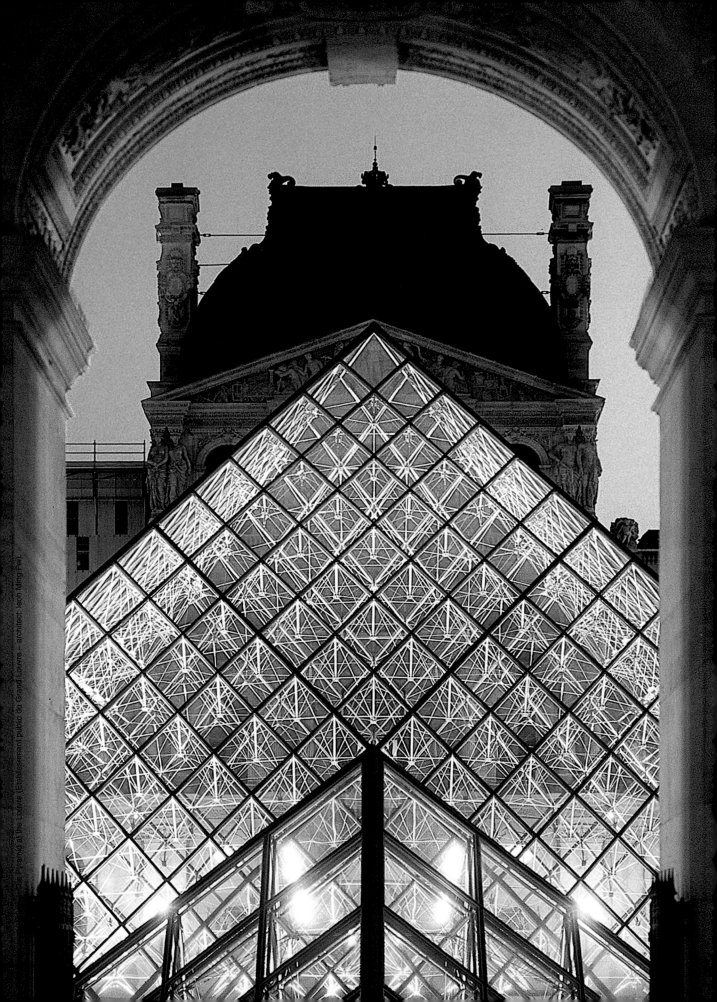

Interior of the museum reception area (Etablissement public du Grand Louvre – architect: Ieoh Ming Pei).

HELLENIC GREEK ART
(late 3rd century – 1st century BC):
"Venus de Milo".

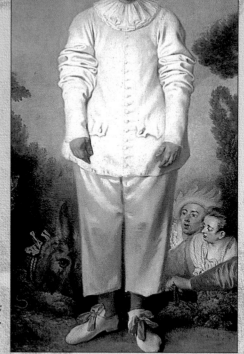

Jean–Antoine WATTEAU (1684–1721):
"Gilles".

EGYPTIAN ART
(c. 2500 BC – 5th dynasty):
"The Seated Scribe".

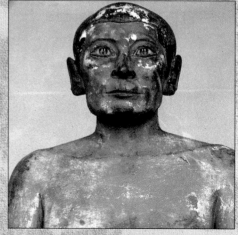

28   Giovanni Battista TIEPOLO (1696–1770): "Jesus Curing the Paralytic".   Jean FOUQUET (1415/1420–1478/1481): "Charles VII".

LEONARDO *da Vinci (1452–1519): "Mona Lisa, la Gioconda".*

Jean Honoré FRAGONARD (1732–1806): "The Bolt".

Sandro FILIPEPI, known as BOTTICELLI (1445–1510): "The Virgin and Child with Five Angels".

ROMAN ANTIQUITIES:
"Statue of Emperor Augustus".

Francisco de GOYA Y LUCIENTES (1746–1828):
"The Countess del Carpio, Marquesa de la Solana".

Georges de LA TOUR (1593–1652): "The Cheat with the Ace of Diamonds".

Frans HALS (1580/1585–1666): "The Bohemian Girl".

Elisabeth VIGEE, Madame VIGEE–LEBRUN (1755–1842):
"The Artist and her Daughter, Jeanne–Lucie".

Jean-Baptiste Camille COROT (1796–1875):
"Bridge at Mantes".

FONTAINEBLEAU SCHOOL (late 15th century):
"Gabrielle d'Estrée and the Duchess of Villars".

Tiziano VECELLIO, known as TITIAN (1488/1490–1576):
"The Virgin and Child, St Stephen, St Ambroise, St Maurice".

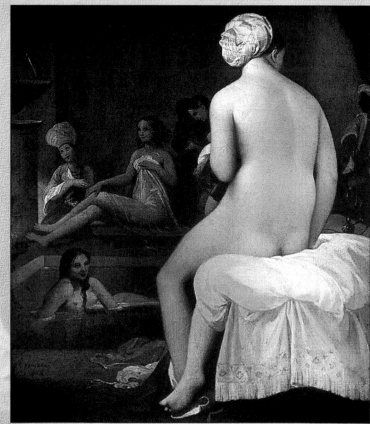

EGYPTIAN ANTIQUITIES (c. 1290–1224 BC):
"Seated Statue of Ramses II".

Jean Auguste Dominique INGRES (1780–1867): "The Young Bather, Harem Interior".

Eugène DELACROIX (1798–1863): "Liberty Guiding the People".

LE NAIN (...Antoine †1648, Louis †1648, Mathieu †1677): "Pilgrims at Emmaus".

Nicolas POUSSIN (1594–1665): "The Shepherds of Arcadia".

Jean CLOUET (1485 ?–1540/1541):
"Portrait of Francis I".

Louis DAVID (1748–1825): "The Oath of the Horatii".

Antoine, Baron GROS (1771–1835): "Bonaparte on the Arcole Bridge".

Antonio PISANO, known as PISANELLO (1395 ?– c. 1455): "Portrait of a Princess of the House of Este".

Claude GELLEE, known as Claude LORRAIN or LE LORRAIN (1600–1682): "Seaport at Sunset".

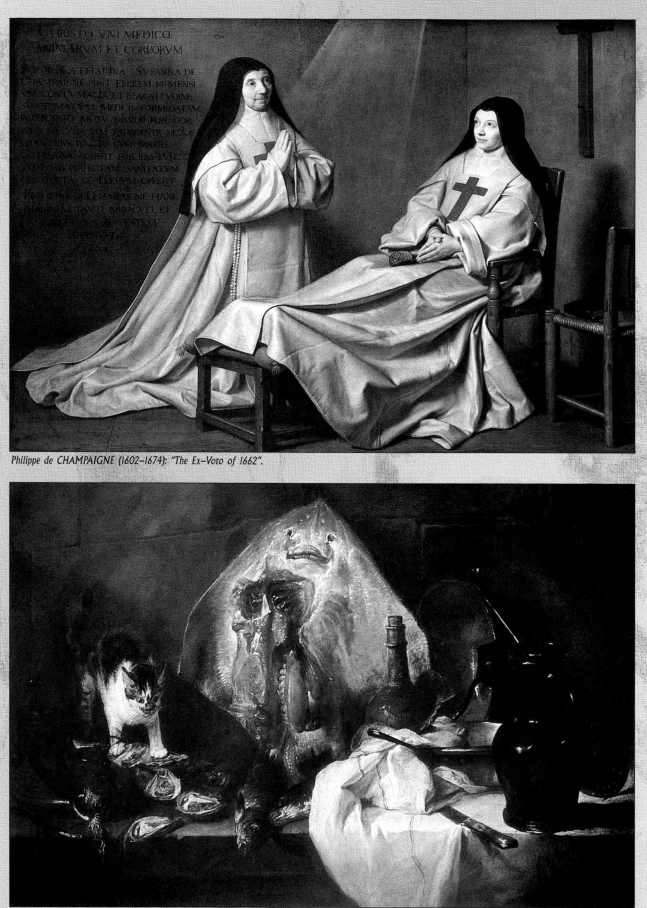

Philippe de CHAMPAIGNE (1602-1674): "The Ex-Voto of 1662".

Jean Siméon CHARDIN (1699-1779): "The Ray".

François BOUCHER (1703–1770): "Diana Leaving her Bath".

The Pyramid at the Louvre (architect: Ieoh Ming Pei – Etablissement public du Grand Louvre).

TUILERIES

The Gardens of the Tuileries, one of the largest public parks in Paris, with its 28 hectares and 2800 trees, retains to this day the appearance given to it by Le Nôtre, the great gardener to King Louis XIV. Besides its lawns and shrubberies, the gardens contain museums - l'Orangerie and Jeu de Paume - and statues - works by Coustou, Coysevox, Carpeaux, Barrois, Barrias, Cain, Maillol and others - making it a kind of open air antechamber to the Louvre museum. Running parallel to the gardens is the rue de Rivoli which was constructed on a commission from Napoleon Bonaparte in 1804. Beneath its arcades are many souvenir shops, cafés and tea rooms for the delight of passers-by and tourists. In the centre, between the Louvre and the Tuileries is Place des Pyramides, where a statue of Joan of Arc by Frémiet is a reminder that the heroine was wounded on this site during an attack to deliver Paris in 1429.

LE NÔTRE

PLACE DE LA CONCORDE

8me ARRt

PLACE DE LA CONCORDE

The largest square in Paris - 84,000 m2 - was laid out between 1754 and 1763 to the plans of the architect Gabriel as the site for the equestrian statue of Louis XV. The statue was removed in 1790, and Place Louis XV renamed Place de la Révolution. On 21 January 1793, a scaffold was erected here for the execution of King Louis XVI, and in two years 1119 of the condemned were guillotined here. In 1795 the site took the name Place de la Concorde, became Place Louis XV again in 1814, then Place Louis XVI in 1826, before reverting to its present name in 1830. In 1836 the engineer Jean-Baptiste Apollinaire Lebas erected an obelisk from the temple of Luxor here, given to King Louis-Philippe in 1831 by the Viceroy of Egypt, Mohamet Ali. This pink syenite monolith, 23 m high and weighing 230 tonnes, stands in the centre of the square between two fountains. Facing the Seine, two houses designed by Gabriel can be admired from either side of the Rue Royale: Hôtel de Crillon on the left and the Ministry of Naval Affairs on the right. Framing the entrance to the Champs Elysées are Guillaume Coustou's Marly horses facing the winged horses of Mercy, Mercury and Fame by Antoine Coysevox, which stand by the gates of the Tuileries Gardens.

The fountains of Place de la Concorde are laid out to designs by Jacques-Ignace Hittorff, to whom we also owe the eighteen plinthed columns between the balustrades as well as the eight statues he was responsible for ordering and which symbolise the cities of Lille, Strasbourg, Lyons, Marseilles, Bordeaux, Nantes, Brest and Rouen, in the four corners of the square.

Bottom left,
the Rond–Point on the Champs Elysées,
designed by Le Nôtre in 1667.

Bottom right,
the Statue of Clémenceau, "The Father of Victory",
by François–Victor Cogné (1932).

Petit Palais (arch. Charles Girault),
a museum housing the City of Paris art collections. ▶

◀ Grand Palais (arch. Deglane, Louvet and Thomas).

Between the Rond-Point and the Place de la Concorde, the Avenue Champs Elysées becomes a place to stroll, as laid down by decree in 1667. Its development was entrusted to Le Nôtre. The green area was enhanced in the 19th century by theatres - known as Panoramas at that time - restaurants, and, at the end of the century, two palaces, the Petit Palais and the Grand Palais, built for the World Fair of 1900 and today museums and art galleries. In our times the Marigny and Renaud-Barrault theatres, l'Espace Pierre-Cardin and the Ledoyen, Pavillon de l'Elysée, Pavillon Gabriel and Laurent restaurants offer hospitality to theatre-goers and enlightened gourmets.

Promenade des Champs Elysées.

Théâtre Marigny, designed by Charles Garnier in 1883.

ARC DE TRIOMPHE

Dominating "the most beautiful avenue in the world", the Arc de Triomphe de l'Etoile stands at the centre of a perspective which starts at the Louvre Palace, passes through the Arc de Triomphe du Carrousel, the Tuileries Gardens and Place de la Concorde to finish at the Grande Arche, in the La Défense district. This work, some 50 m high and 40 m wide, was constructed by a decree of Napoleon 1 of 18 February 1806. The architect Jean-François Chalgrin was entrusted with its completion, which was accomplished in 1836. The monument, dedicated to the glory of the imperial armies, is decorated with some famous high reliefs on the four pillars: "Departure of the volunteers of 1792" or "la Marseillaise" by François Rude, "the Triumph of 1810" by Jean-Pierre Cortot, and "Peace" and "Resistance" by Antoine Etex. The stone is also engraved with the names of the greatest victories of the Republic and the Empire together with the names of 558 generals. The ashes of Napoleon I passed beneath its vaulted arch in 1840, as did the mortal remains of Victor Hugo in 1885 and victorious soldiers on 14 July 1919. In memory of the dead of the Great War, the body of the Unknown Soldier was laid to rest here on 11 November 1920 on whose Tomb burns a flame which is rekindled each evening.

Conceived by Colbert following a decree by Louis XIV, the Tuileries walk took the name Champs Elysées [Elysian Fields] in 1694. Three centuries later major works gave the famous avenue all the majesty the minister of the Sun King wished for. A triumphal way, a place for strolling, or an obligatory route for Heads of State on official visits, the Champs Elysées is also the prestigious shop-window of Paris. The 628 buildings lining the service roads include cinemas, luxury shops, cafés, restaurants, banks, motor manufacturers and airlines, vying with each other in imagination to give the avenue its glamour and enhance the capital's reputation.

The Arc de Triomphe de l'Etoile from Avenue Foch.

8me ARR.

AVENUE DES CHAMPS·ÉLYSÉES

La Grande Arche (architect: Johan Otto von Spreckelsen); right, the CNIT (architects: Camelot, de Mailly and Zehrfuss).

LA DEFENSE

In the 18th century King Louis XV wished to link the Louvre to the palace at Versailles and thus extend the royal route carved out by Le Nôtre. By the end of his reign, after passing through Neuilly and crossing the Seine, the road reached the knoll of Chantecoq where a great intersection was laid out. Later a statue of Napoleon in its centre was taken down in 1870 and replaced in 1883 by a bronze group by Louis-Ernest Barrias, "la Défense de Paris", commemorating Parisian resistance to the Prussian siege during the winter of 1870-1871. The statue gave its name to the site which has been developed in the communes of Puteaux and Courbevoie. Various office and residential property developments, conceived from 1950 onwards, have resulted in the townscape we see today: tower blocks, the highest of which reach some hundred metres, the CNIT building (1958), the Quatre Temps shopping centre (1981), and the Grande Arche (1989). This monument in the shape of a hollow 110 m cube, weighing 300,000 tonnes, is the work of the Danish architect Johan Otto von Spreckelsen. On the esplanade, in addition to lines of trees, the works of some sixty artists can be seen, forming an open air museum of modern art. Amongst them are Alexandre Calder's "Stabile" and Juan Miró's "Personnages". Today the area has 30,000 residents and 100,000 people come here to work each day.

Between the pillars of the Grande Arche, the "Sail" by the engineer Peter Rice.

BOIS DE BOULOGNE

Château de Longchamp.

ROUTE
DE LA
GRANDE CASCADE

Longchamp racecourse.

Monument des Fusillés.

The lower lake.

Château de Bagatelle.

Châlet des Iles.

PARC DE MONCEAU

Once the property of the seigneury of Clichy, in the 18th century the Mousseaux site was acquired in lots by a few lords and financiers of the period. Here they constructed buildings known as "follies". Amongst them, "Folie de Chartres", the property of Louis-Philippe of Orleans who, having bought the land in 1769, had Carmontelle construct a garden of illusions in 1778, scattered with "fabriques" ['creations'] of which some still survive today: the "Naumachie", the "Egyptian pyramid " and others. On 22 October 1797 Garnerin made the first parachute drop from a balloon floating 1000 m above the ground. The city of Paris became owners of the site in 1870 and Napoleon III later asked Alphand to remodel the 8.5 h grounds giving it the appearance it has today. The entrances, from the avenues Van Dick and Velasquez, are protected by magnificent gates, the work of Davioud. On the Boulevard Malesherbes, Avenue Velasquez side, the Cernuschi museum houses a collection of Chinese art.

QUARTIER DE L'EUROPE

House of Monsieur Loo. Fernand Block built this residence between 1926 and 1928 for a Chinese antiquarian, Ching Tsai Loo, who turned it into a gallery devoted to Asian art.

St-Augustin church: beneath its stone mantle, Victor Baltard concealed a metal structure supporting the interior of the church, built between 1860 and 1871.

Gare Saint-Lazare, terminus of the first railway line opened in 1837, later removed to its present site in 1841. The buildings, constructed by Alfred Armand and fitted out by Juste Lisch for the 1889 World Fair, are a terminus for trains travelling to and from Normandy.

Chapelle Expiatoire, built between 1815 and 1826 by the architect Fontaine, commissioned by Louis XVIII, occupies the site of the former cemetery of la Madeleine de la Ville l'Evêque, in which around 3000 victims of the Revolution were buried. Among them, Louis XVI and Marie-Antoinette, whose remains were transferred to the Saint-Denis basilica in 1815.

Cercle National des Armées, built in 1927 by Charles Lemaresquier on the site of the former Pépinière barracks.

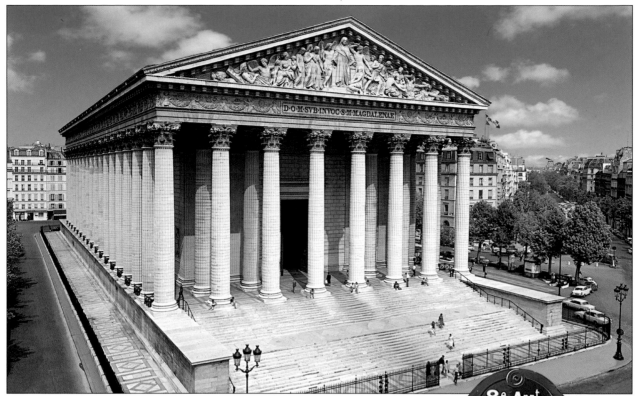

MADELEINE

Dedicated in 1492 by King Charles VIII to St Mary-Magdalen "who, from time immemorial, has been especially honoured in the borough", over the years a succession of buildings was to see the light of day, culminating in the present church, whose construction was decided by Napoleon I in 1806. The building, whose plans were commissioned by Pierre-Alexandre Vignon, were to be consecrated to the glory of the Great Army and the architecture inspired by Greek temples. Louis XVIII continued the works in accordance with the original plans, but the temple, completed in 1842, was used for worship. Supported by 52 Corinthian columns, the building's triangular façade presents the "Last Judgment" by the sculptor Philippe-Henri Lemaire. Intersecting with Rue Royale, made famous by a certain well-known restaurant, the street of Faubourg Saint-Honoré is the home of numerous boutiques selling haute couture and internationally famous luxury goods.

Madeleine gallery (1845).

PLACE VENDOME

From an idea of the minister, Louvois, the architect Jules Hardouin-Mansart designed the square completed in 1720 to be surrounded by buildings with identical façades. At the centre of Place des Conquêtes, later renamed place Louis-le-Grand, there stood until 1792 an equestrian statue of Louis XIV, the work of Girardon. It was replaced in 1806 by a column inspired by the Trajan Column in Rome on the orders of Napoleon I. The bronze plaques illustrating the campaign of 1805 were made from melting down 1200 cannons captured at the battle of Austerlitz. A statue of the Emperor crowned the edifice which was knocked down on the orders of Gustave Courbet during the Commune in 1871. It was re-erected at the painter's expense in 1873.

OPERA

Following the attack on Napoleon III perpetrated by Orsini on 14 January 1858, the Emperor decided to construct a new opera house for Paris. Charles Garnier, winner of a competition which attracted 171 entries, began work in 1861. It was officially opened on 5 January 1875 under Mac-Mahon's presidency. A real architectural masterpiece of the Second Empire, the Opéra is sumptuously decorative. Raised above a wide terrace with ten steps, seven fully-arched arcades flanked by sculpted groups, including "la Danse" by Jean-Baptiste Carpeaux, open into the lobbies. On the first floor, a loggia with eight double Corinthian pillars in Ravières stone opens into the foyer, echoing the small columns that frame the window openings surmounted with gilded bronze busts of composers. An attic storey dominates the loggia, edged with 53 antique masks in gilded bronze linked by a garland and sculpted by Jean-Baptiste Klagmann. Above, two groups in bronze by Charles-Alphonse Gumery, symbolising Harmony on the right and Poetry on the left. Finally, the dome in copper verdigris heightened with gold and surmounted by a composition by Aimé Millet "Apollo between Dance and Music raising the golden lyre above his head with both hands".

Main staircase.

Orchestra pit and main curtain.

Fountain beneath the small rotunda.

General view of the auditorium from the stage.

The great chandelier and the ceiling of the auditorium painted by Marc Chagall.

Inside the building the same profusion of materials, decoration and colour is to be found. This desire to achieve grandeur is successfully confirmed in the magnificent grand staircase which is divided in two in front of the orchestra entrance. The main foyer is richly decorated with columns, statues, lamps and allegorical paintings by Paul Baudry. The auditorium, despite the size of the building with a floor area of 110,000 m², has an audience capacity of only 2158. From the ceiling, since 1964 covered by a painting by Marc Chagall, hangs a massive lamp designed by Garnier himself. The fore-stage curtain, appearing to be a red velvet drape decorated with gold braid, is in fact a 'trompe l'oeil' painting by Auguste Alfred Rubé and Philippe Chaperon. Behind it, the Italianate stage is approximately 1200 m² permitting up to 450 performers on stage at any one time; the dancers' greenroom, communicating with it, is decorated with paintings by Boulanger, and the back wall is fitted with mirrors. Legend has it that an underground river, la Grange Batelière, flows beneath the Opéra.

The main foyer.

The dancers' greenroom.

The Opéra, the national academy of music and dance [Académie de Musique et de Danse], is a place of wonder and marvels, full of the passions expressed here - for art and life - in a kind of temple, where the world finds itself recreated through singing and dancing. Composers and choreographers, instrumentalists, distinguished singers and star dancers have performed here, at the height of their talent, sometimes achieving the sublime and sometimes falling to the depths of despair. Here the most spectacular plots of a Romanesque world have been hatched or unravelled, on stage, in the auditorium and the boxes, adorned with the finest worldly glories, in the corridors of this fabled palace.

In the Place de l'Opéra, at the corner of Boulevard des Capucines, the terrace of the Café de la Paix is reputed to be the largest in Paris. It has always, since the Second Empire, been an international meeting place for the literary, artistic and political world. ▼

ST-EUSTACHE CHURCH

The construction of Saint-Eustache church on the site of a chapel dedicated to St Agnes began in 1532. The building, consecrated in 1637, has the highest nave in Paris. The plan of the interior is similar to that of Notre-Dame. Remarkable acoustics permit the organ - 85 stops, 7000 pipes - to give of its best. A special feature of the church is that it contains the greatest number of famous sepulchres. Still to be seen today is Colbert's tomb, sculpted by Coysevox and Tuby, to Le Brun's designs. The former parish of the corporations of Les Halles is today dominated by Forum des Halles, a commercial, cultural and leisure complex completed in 1986.

The Fountain of the Innocents, constructed by the sculptor Jean Goujon between 1547 and 1549, commissioned, it is thought, by Philippe Auguste. It stands at the corner of Rue Saint–Denis and Rue Berger (formerly Rue aux Fers).

FORUM DES HALLES

The Forum des Halles, a vast quadrilateral in the shape of an inverted pyramid is the work of architects Claude Vasconi and Georges Penchréac'h. Spread over four levels are numerous shops, as well a large multiplex cinema.

CENTRE POMPIDOU

In December 1969 President Georges Pompidou decided to establish a museum devoted to modern art which he wanted to be accessible to the greatest possible number of people. The plans of architects Renzo Piano and Richard Rogers, assisted by G. Franchini, were selected in 1971 and have resulted in an original construction where the interior space is totally usable and adaptable, since the functional elements -"the pipes"- have all been banished to the exterior. The building consists of a 15,000 tonne metal framework, housing the collections of the modern art museum, a library, various performance and conference rooms, an industrial design centre and the I.R.C.A.M. [Institut de Recherche et Coordination Acoustique/Musique - an institute for research and development in contemporary music]. An obligatory stop for package tourists, 8 million people every year visit the Centre National d'Art et de Culture Georges Pompidou.

St-Merri church, rebuilt between 1515 and 1612, has a remarkable interior and houses the oldest bell in Paris (1331).

▼

HOTEL DE VILLE

The present Renaissance-style building, was reconstructed by Ballu and Deperthes on the model of the former building, devastated by the flames of the Paris Commune in 1871. It had been designed by "Il Boccoro" for François I, and succeeded the former "Maison aux Pilliers" [Pillared House] acquired in 1357 by Etienne Marcel to house the Municipal Assembly.

4° Arr!

PLACE
DE L'HÔTEL
DE VILLE

61

MARAIS

In the heart of the Marais, a favoured district in which numerous lords took up residence from the 15th century, is the Place des Vosges, consisting of 36 brick and free-stone houses arranged around a quadrangle. Building began in 1605 on the orders of Henri IV and it was officially opened in 1612 under the name Place Royale. It took the name Place des Vosges in 1800, to honour the département of that name whose citizens were the first to pay their taxes. The house inhabited by Victor Hugo in the last century can be seen at No. 6, now converted into a museum.

3ᵉ Arrᵗ

PLACE DES VOSGES

Notre–Dame des Blancs Manteaux church, rebuilt in 1685 on plans by Dom Antoine de Machy, takes its name from the white cloaks worn by the mendicant order of the Serfs of the Virgin, whose monastery stood on this site. The interior contains a remarkable German pulpit (1749) made of wood inlaid with ivory and pewter marquetry.

The old houses on rue François Miron are reminiscent of the Middle Ages. Presumed to be 15th century, they were restored in 1967.

Standing behind the elm where justice was dispensed, is the classical façade (1616–1621) of the Saint-Gervais–Saint–Protais church, begun in 1494 in Flamboyant Gothic style. The organ (17th–18th century) was for many generations in the charge of the Couperin family.

Hôtel de Sens: Tristan de Salazar, Bishop of Sens, had this mansion built between 1475 and 1519. It is an example of Parisian medieval architecture, in spite of significant restorations. Since 1961, it has housed the Forney Library, specialising in decorative arts, crafts and industrial techniques (collections of posters, wallpapers, periodicals...).

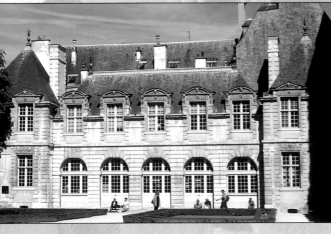

Hôtel de Sully: its most illustrious owner, Maximilien de Béthune, Duc de Sully, Armes minister of Henri IV bought it in 1634 and left it his name. It was originally built for the financial controller Mesme Gallet, by Jean Androuet du Cerceau, around 1625, in the spirit of the Renaissance. Abandoned in the 19th century, it was later bought by the State, which restored it in an exemplary fashion. It is now the headquarters of the Centre des Monuments Nationaux.

Hôtel de Lamoignon, built in the 16th century by Henri II for his legitimate daughter, Diane of France, Duchess of Angoulême, is named after the first president of the Parliament of Paris.
The Bibliothèque Historique de la Ville de Paris [City of Paris History Library], heir to the legacy of Antoine Moriau in 1759, has been housed here since 1968.

Hôtel de Soubise: François de Rohan, Prince of Soubise, acquired the Hôtel de Guise in 1700 and entrusted its transformation to Pierre–Alexis Delamain. This magnificent residence, whose apartments are open to visitors, has housed the Musée de l'Histoire de France since 1867.

Hôtel Hérouet: the building, badly damaged by bombing in August 1944 and since rebuilt, only faintly resembles the mansion built in the early 16th century for a king's counsellor to Parliament.

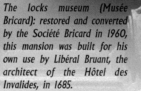

The locks museum (Musée Bricard): restored and converted by the Société Bricard in 1960, this mansion was built for his own use by Libéral Bruant, the architect of the Hôtel des Invalides, in 1685.

Hôtel Carnavalet: built in 1548 for Jacques de Ligneris, the mansion was taken over in 1578 by the widow of François de Kernevenoy, renamed Carnavalet by the people of Paris. Claude Boislève bought it in 1654 and commissioned François Mansart to embellish it. From 1677 to 1696, the Marquise de Sévigné was its illustrious tenant. Owned by the City of Paris since 1866, the capital tells its own story here through the Musée de l'Histoire de Paris.

Hôtel de Clisson: of the mansion built around 1375 by the constable Olivier de Clisson only this door remains, a unique example of 14th century civil architecture in Paris. Bought in 1553 by the Guise family, it kept that name until 1688, on the death of the last descendent, Marie.

Hôtel Aubert de Fontenay – known as Hôtel Salé: built in 1656 by Jean Boullier de Bourges for Pierre Aubert de Fontenay, the name probably derives from his job as salt–tax collector. The building now houses the Musée Picasso, which opened in 1985.

BERCY - BASTILLE

Place de la Bastille, view from the Arsenal marina.

Parc de Bercy.

Palais Omnisport [Sports Centre] at Paris−Bercy, the facilities inside are designed for both sport-ing events and variety shows (architects Andrault, Guvan and Parat).

The July column, topped by the "Spirit of Liberty", by Dumont, this work by Alavoine rises to a height of over 50 m. Louis−Philippe, when unveiling it in 1840, wished to commemorate the victims of the "Trois Glorieuses" (the three−day Revolution of 27−28−29 July 1830), to which were later added those of 1848, all of them buried in the foundations of the monument.

Wishing to improve water distribution in Paris and the movement of boats between the lower and upper Seine, a law was passed on 29 Floreal year X (1802) specifying the layout of the canals.

The Saint-Martin canal was started twenty years later, under the supervision of Charles-Eduoard de Villiers and the engineers Tarbé and Brémentier, and officially opened on 4 November 1825. Beginning at the Villette basin, it flows in the open for 2.431 km with a width of 27 m and draught of 1.90 m; from La Douane footbridge it runs underground for 2.123 km before again finding itself in the open in the Port de l'Arsenal - now a yacht marina - before rejoining the Seine. Five bridges, five footbridges, three swing bridges and nine locks add to the charm of its towpaths which are very popular with walkers.

Not far away, in the centre of the square of the same name, is the statue of the Republic, the work of the brothers Léopold and Charles Morice, unveiled on 14 July 1883.

BUTTES CHAUMONT

On the site of some disused gypsum quarries which had been worked since the 13th century, in 1863 Baron Haussmann decided to create a park, the plans for which he entrusted to the engineer Alphand. This pleasure garden, backing on to the "Mont Chauve" mound - today Buttes Chaumont - has a lake at its centre, in the middle of which is a promontory surmounted by a Greek monopteral temple, the work of Davioud. Two bridges link it to the shore, one of brick 22 m above the water and the other a suspension bridge 65 m long. A grotto was created at the entrance to one of the old quarries, decorated with mock stalactites and a waterfall 30 m high. A café-restaurant and some snack-bars have been built in the park in which many species of trees planted by Barillet-Deschamps in 1866 still stand.

La Villette rotunda, the remains of 54 tax offices built by Claude–Nicolas Ledoux in the late 18th century.

THE CITE DES SCIENCES ET DE L'INDUSTRIE

The Cité des sciences et de l'industrie, Paris's museum of science and industry, is an immense parallelepiped standing to the north of the Ourq canal in La Villette park, and at 100,000 m² Europe's biggest institution popularising science and technology. Constructed from former abattoir buildings, the main structure of la Cité des sciences was designed by the architect Adrien Fainsilber, together with the glittering Geode sphere facing it. A genuine resource for

learning about the great scientific and technological advances of our day, when the Cité des sciences was officially opened in 1986 it inaugurated a new concept for science museums. Through its many activities it transports the visitor to a world combining knowledge and the joys of discovery. This world is made up of many different places - the permanent and temporary exhibitions at the Explora museum and its planetarium; the Cité des enfants [Children's City] for 3 to 12 year-olds; Cyber-base, a space offering introductory and advanced courses in web surfing as well as information and communication technologies; the media library, open to everyone, offers books, magazines, educational software, CD Roms...; the Cité des métiers, the Cité de la santé. In the park, there are the Geode and its spectacular shows, the Cinaxe and its simulation cabin and the undersea Argonaute.

SACRE-COEUR BASILICA

In the 17th century, Sister Marguerite-Marie, a humble nun, was chosen by Our Lord to ask France to erect a monument "to the glory of his Divine Heart". There was a wait of two centuries before two devout Christians, Alexandre-Félix Legentil and his brother-in-law Hubert Rohault de Fleury, vowed, in December 1870, to build a church dedicated to the Sacred Heart, in answer to the wish expressed by Christ.

With a large following of the faithful, the approval of Monseignor Guilbert, Archbishop of Paris and the blessing of Pope Pius IX, l'Oeuvre du Voeu National [Works of the National Vow] was adopted on 25 July 1873 by the National Assembly. The cost of construction, which rose to more than forty million francs, was to be paid by the faithful through an initial subscription allowing each subscriber to buy one stone, including some which, depending on how much had been paid, gave the right for it to be inscribed with the donor's initials. The plans of Paul Abadie were selected and the first stone was laid on 18 June 1875 in the presence of Marshal MacMahon, President of the Republic. The basilica was to be officially opened on 28 June 1889, but was not consecrated until 16 October 1919. Meanwhile, Honoré Daumet, Charles Laisné, Henri Rauline, Lucien Magne and Louis-Jean Hulot supervised the realisation of the initial plans, interpreting and sometimes radically altering them. The building, 85 m long, 35 m wide and 83.33 m high, was constructed in Château-Landon stone, which on contact with rainwater secretes a white substance, lime, and gives the building its unsullied appearance. Inspired by the Roman-Byzantine style, it comprises a vast central rotunda, around which a short nave, two transepts and a chancel are laid out to form the arms of a cross. On the façade, constructed in the image of the Romanesque churches of the Charentes, and above the pediment, Gustave Michel's statue of the Sacred Heart can be seen. On either side of the porch are the equestrian statues of St Joan of Arc and St Louis, cast by Hippolyte Lefebvre.

Interior of the Sacré–Coeur basilica: top left, the statue of Sacré–Coeur d'Argent, by Eugène Benet; the solid silver statue of the Holy Virgin holding her son, made by Paul Brunet in 1876 (top right); below, the great organ of Aristide Cavaillé–Coll, constructed in 1898: 78 stops – 4 keyboards of which three are enclosed.

Opposite: the mosaic laid to the drawings of Marcel Magne and Luc–Olivier Merson. Covering an area of 475 m², it represents the Sacred Heart of Jesus glorified by the Catholic Church and France. ▶

PLACE DU TERTRE

From the 14th century, the Place du Tertre was owned by Montmartre Abbey which had its whipping post there. In the 18th century it became the heart of the Montmartre commune, which in 1790 was the site of the first town hall, at No. 3. This house was the residence of the first mayor, Félix Desportes de Blinval. The commune was then annexed to Paris in 1860, by a decree issued by Baron Haussmann. Nevertheless, the site preserved its village and bohemian appearance and attracted large numbers of artists including Corot, Delacroix, Géricault, Degas, Renoir, Cézanne, Manet, Van Gogh and Toulouse-Lautrec amongst others, who depicted the atmosphere of Montmartre in their work. In our day, the square is still popular with painters, portrait artists and caricaturists, who, with the many cafés, restaurants and cabarets, create that special Montmartre atmosphere: no-one knows Paris if he has not climbed "la butte".

A general view of the Sacré-Coeur basilica; on the left the funicular railway which climbs the 45 m incline and links Place Saint-Pierre and Rue Saint-Eleuthère (cabins designed by R. Talon - station architect: F. Deslaugiers). ▼

TOURING-CLUB DE FRANCE

COMMUNE LIBRE
du vieux
MONTMARTRE

DON DUNLOP

MONTMARTRE

Amongst the cabarets which make the name of Montmartre is the well-known "Lapin Agile" at No. 22 Rue des Saules at the corner of Rue Saint-Vincent. In 1860 it was a notorious dance hall called "Au rendez-vous des voleurs" [Thieves' meeting place] then "Cabaret des assassins" [Murderers' Cabaret] at the period when Salz became its owner. In 1886, a former cancan dancer, Adèle Decerf, acquired it and renamed the place "Ma campagne" [My Country]. Aristide Bruant bought the property in 1903 and entrusted its management to Frédéric Gérard - "Le père Frédé". Meanwhile the famous rabbit sign painted by the cartoonist André Gill had given the establishment the name by which we know it today.

MOULIN ROUGE

At the foot of the mount, "between Pigalle and Blanche", Boulevard de Clichy shamelessly flaunts its unique establishments, popular with night-time revellers. Amongst the boutiques, cafés, cinemas and cabarets, every night the Moulin Rouge marks the parade by turning its illuminated sails. Opened on 6 October 1889, the Moulin Rouge dance hall rapidly became very successful. Special attractions were also offered to its audience, the most famous of which was the "quadrille naturaliste", danced by colourful figures such as La Goulue, Jane Avril and Valentin-le-Désossé, who were to be immortalised by the pencil of Henri de Toulouse-Lautrec. After several refurbishments at the beginning of the century, the establishment came to specialise in revues: that of 1927 "Ça c'est Paris" [That's Paris], led by Mistinguett, was a triumph. In 1937, the dance hall was converted into a night club, ultra-modern for its time. Edith Piaf and Yves Montand appeared here in July 1944. The establishment was refurbished again in 1951 by Henri Mahé, and again in 1959 with the creation of the "dinner-show", finally in 1962 the dancers turned mermaids performed for the first time in a giant aquarium. Throughout its history, the Moulin Rouge dance hall has attracted glittering audiences, notably members of the British royal family, as well as leading artists from each period. Today it is still a venue popular with lovers of music-hall.

The French Cancan, the proper original version, was danced for the first time in 1889 at the Moulin Rouge. This dance, based on the quadrille, had a success that knew no borders and it was on the other side of the Channel that Englishman Charles Morton gave it the name by which it is still known today. Well over a century old, this wild dance still reveals to the audience the legs of the prettiest girls of Paris... and elsewhere!

Notre–Dame Cathedral, viewed from the Pont de l'Archevêché.

Saint–Julien Le Pauvre church.   *Rue du Chat qui Pèche.*

JARDIN DES PLANTES

The Jardin des Plantes, originally the "royal garden of medicinal herbs", was founded in 1626 by Héroard and Guy de la Brosse, doctors to King Louis XIII. Buffon, appointed steward in 1739, laid it out and developed the interest in the natural sciences by surrounding himself with a great many academics, such as Jussieu, Daubenton and others. By decree of the Convention, the garden later became the national natural history museum in 1793. The gardens are planted with numerous plant species - including the famous Cedar of Lebanon smuggled back by Jussieu in 1734; they also contain a menagerie and exhibition galleries: geology, mineralogy, botany, anatomy and comparative palaeontology and zoology.

Coming down from Place de la Contrescarpe, Rue Mouffetard and its lively, picturesque market on the forecourt of Saint–Médard church.

PANTHEON

Dedicated to Sainte Geneviève, the royal church designed by Jacques-Germain Soufflot, commissioned by Louis XV, was completed in 1790. One year later, the Revolution made it the last resting place of "grand hommes" [great men], the Panthéon. Napoleon yielded it to the church in 1806, but in 1830, Louis-Philippe converted the building back into a Pantheon, which became the Temple d'Humanité in 1848 and the National Basilica in 1853, in the name of St Geneviève. The Third Republic again converted it back into a Pantheon for the funeral of Victor Hugo on 1 June 1885. The building is constructed in the shape a Greek cross 110 m long by 84.50 m wide and 83 m high. The monumental portico supports the triangular pediment carved by Pierre-Jean David d'Angers and bears the inscription in gold lettering: "Aux grand hommes la Patrie reconnaissante" [To great men, their grateful country]. Inside, the dome is decorated with a fresco by Antoine-Jean Gros depicting the ascension of St Geneviève. It was here that Foucault conducted his pendulum experiments in 1851. In the necropolis lie the remains of some sixty distinguished people, among them Sadi Carnot, Emile Zola and Jean Jaurès.

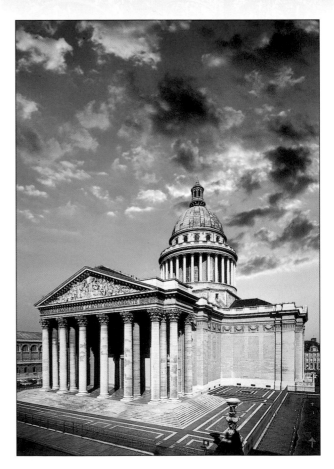

LUXEMBOURG PALACE AND GARDENS

It was François of Luxembourg, Prince of Tingry, who gave his name to the building - the present Petit Luxembourg - by acquiring it in 1570. Marie de Médicis bought it in 1612, together with the surrounding land, and had a palace to suit her built by Salomon de Brosse, while conserving the original residence. The property then passed through the hands of: Gaston d'Orléans, Mademoiselle de Montpensier, the Duchess of Guise, Madame de Maintenon, Philippe d'Orléans, the Duchess of Berry and the Count of Provence, who all lived there. Bonaparte granted the building to the Senate in 1800, and it became the Chambre des Pairs [equivalent of the House of Lords] under the Restoration. From the Third Republic, the Luxembourg again housed the Senate. The French classical-style garden was commissioned by Marie de Médicis. It is adorned with fountains and some fifty statues, those of the terrace representing the queens of France and illustrious ladies.

HOTEL DE CLUNY

In the heart of the Latin Quarter, Cluny is evidence of the origins
of the capital: the Gallo-Roman baths, constructed in the late 2nd and early
3rd centuries, to which the Hôtel de Cluny is attached, a rare example of
civic architecture of the late Middle Ages. Today the entire building is a
national museum, established by an Act passed on 24 July 1843. The baths
proper occupy a quadrangle some 100 m long by 65 m wide, and are built
to the traditional Roman bathing sequence: a room for exercising before
bathing communicating with the central frigidarium - this room, 14.50 m in
height, is remarkable both for its exceptional state of preservation and for
the presence of consoles with the motif of the prow of a merchant ship, a
symbol attributed to the corporation of Nautes - this in turn opens on to
the tepidarium (for warm individual baths) and the caldarium for hot baths.
The Hôtel de Cluny, constructed by Jacques d'Amboise, elder brother of
the Louis XII's cardinal and minister and Abbot of Cluny from 1485 to 1510,
today houses a collection of medieval art.

SAINT-MICHEL

Under the Second Empire, Baron Haussmann, wishing to orient the Boulevard Saint-Michel into the perspective of the view from Sainte-Chapelle, had the north-south road diverted from its axis. As the view was then obstructed by the gable wall of the buildings at the corner of Rue Danton, he had the idea of covering this with a decorative fountain. The monument, the work of the sculptor Gabriel Davioud, was unveiled on 5 August 1860. Measuring 26 m high and 15 m wide, the fountain is formed from four large bowls superimposed in steps, flanked by two crouching winged dragons. In the central recess, surrounded by four Corinthian columns of Languedoc red marble, stands the bronze statue of "St Michael defeating the dragon" by Francisque-Joseph Duret. Above, the polychromatic marble attic is ornamented with four statues symbolising "Prudence", "Strength", "Justice" and "Temperance". At the apex, the pediment is broken by an escutcheon embellished with a helmet and a sceptre, flanked by Auguste Debay's allegorical "Power" and "Moderation".

On 15 Prairial in the year XIII, by a decision of Minister Champagny, the site of the former church of Saint-André-des-Arts became a square of the same name. The church itself, built in the 13th century and commissioned by the Abbot of Saint-Germain, was remarkable both architecturally and for its sculptures. Having become the property of the state, the church was sold on 4 Fructidor in the year V (21 August 1797) and demolished a short time later.

SAINT-GERMAIN DES PRES

According to legend, King Childebert I, on the advice of Germain, Bishop of Paris, in 542 had a basilica constructed to house the treasures he had brought back from Saragossa: St Vincent's tunic, a gold Toledo cross and many precious objects. The Merovingian kings were buried here, as was St Germain in 576. After being pillaged by the Normans in 845, the basilica, which had been endowed with a monastery, was demolished in the 9th century. On its foundations Abbot Morard built a Romanesque church, of which the steeple porch constructed between 990 and 1014, still retains a considerable proportion of its original features. Inside, are to be found the tombstones of Descartes, Montfaucon and Mabillon.

Built in 1699, Rue de Furstenberg takes its name from the Cardinal, Abbot of Saint-Germain-des-Prés.

SAINT-SULPICE

The first church dedicated to St Sulpice was built in about 1211 on the site of the present church. When it became too small, Anne of Austria decided in 1646 to have a larger building constructed to the plans of Christophe Gamart, which was to be enlarged again by Le Vau in 1649. The building was not officially opened until 1745. The façade, which we owe to J.N. Servandoni, is flanked by two towers, the work of Chalgrin, one 73 m high and the other 68 m, which remains unfinished. Claude Chappe installed two telegraphs here, which were removed in 1850. The interior has a white marble obelisk and a copper-plated sundial permitting calculation of the dates of the March equinox and Easter Sunday.

Pont des Arts

MUSEE D'ORSAY

The Orleans railway company, wishing to take its lines further into Paris, acquired the site occupied by the Orsay Palace, destroyed during the Paris Commune in 1871. The station and its hotel, built by Victor Laloux, were officially opened on 14 July 1900. A ministerial committee in 1977 converted the buildings into a museum dedicated to the art of the second half of the 19th century. Opened in 1986, the Musée d'Orsay - exterior designed by Renaud Bardon, Pierre Colboc and Jean-Paul Philippon, and interior by Gae Aulenti - houses collections of paintings, sculpture, architecture and town planning, from 1848 to 1914.

Auguste RENOIR (1841–1919): "The Reading".

Edouard MANET (1832–1883): "On the Beach".

Vincent VAN GOGH (1853–1890): "Portrait of Doctor Gachet".

Gustave CAILLEBOTTE (1848–1894): "Rooftops in the snow".

Camille PISSARRO (1830–1903): "The Village Steeple".

Alfred SISLEY (1839–1899): "The Canal du Loing".

Henri de TOULOUSE-LAUTREC (1864–1901): "Jane Avril Dancing".

Henri de TOULOUSE-LAUTREC (1864–1901): "Woman Combing Her Hair".

Paul CEZANNE (1839–1906): "The Card Players".

Edgar DEGAS (1834–1917):
"Women Ironing".

Edouard MANET (1832–1883):
"Woman with Fans
Nina de Callias".

Edgar DEGAS (1834–1917): *Dancing Class*.

Jean–Baptiste Camille COROT (1796–1875): "Ville d'Avray, the Cabassud Houses".

Vincent VAN GOGH (1853–1890): "Church at Auvers–sur–Oise".

Camille PISSARRO (1830–1903): "Woman Hanging the Washing".

PALAIS BOURBON

Louise-Françoise de Bourbon, legitimate daughter of Louis XIV and Madame de Montespan, had the palace which bears her name constructed between 1722 and 1728. Louis XV was its owner in 1756, the Prince de Condé in 1764. In the meantime, the building underwent a number of alterations, until 1791 when the Bourbon Palace became the property of the nation. The Council of the Five Hundred held its first session there on 21 January 1798, as the legislative body of the Empire subsequently did. Since 1814 the Palace, now the Assemblée Nationale [French National Assembly] has housed the Chambre des Députés [Chamber of Deputies - the lower house]. The main façade, the work of Poyet, looks over Place de la Concorde, and is reflected at the end of Rue Royale in the church of the Madeleine. The tympanum, sculpted in 1842 by J.P. Cortot, represents France surrounded by Liberty and Order.

Constructed between 1897 and 1900, Pont Alexandre III, the work of the engineer Jean Résal, was to symbolise the Franco-Russian friendship instigated by Tsar Alexander III and President Sadi Carnot. The first stone was laid on 7 October 1896 in the presence of Tsar Nicholas II, son of Alexander III and the President of the Republic, Félix Faure. Richly decorated, the 40 m wide bridge supports on the keystone of the vault of the arch, two embossed copper fronted motifs by the sculptor Georges Récipon: the arms of Paris surrounded by Seine nymphs upstream, the arms of Russia and the figure of la Néva surrounded by his nymphs downstream. At each end, two square pylons are surmounted by gilded bronze equestrian groups symbolising Pegasus held by Fame. The work, lit by two rows of fourteen three-lamp candelabras, is the finishing touch to the view of the Hôtel des Invalides.

INVALIDES

Louis XIV, moved by seeing his glorious soldiers condemned until then to beg for their bread and to stretch out their mutilated bodies on Pont Neuf, decided in 1670 to found the Hôtel des Invalides. This was built between 1671 to 1676 to the plans of the architect Libéral Bruant, and the work was supervised by Louvois, Minister of War. The main façade, 196 m long, extends from both sides of a huge portal, embellished with an equestrian statue of Louis XIV by Guillaume Coustou. Today the buildings house the Musée de l'Armée, the Musée de l'Artillerie, the Musée des Plans-Reliefs [the Army, Artillery and Relief Map museums] and the military authorities of Paris. The soldiers' church, dedicated to St Louis, was deemed too small by the Sun King and was enlarged by Jules Hardouin-Mansart to whom we owe the current church of the Dôme, completed in 1708. In its crypt rest the ashes of

Napoleon I, brought back from the island of St Helena by the Prince de Joinville in 1840. The sarcophagus of red porphyry from Finland, made by Visconti, contains six coffins of which the last contains the remains of the Emperor. In front is his statue in Coronation dress, beneath a slab is the body of his son, the King of Rome, brought back to France in 1940 on the orders of Adolf Hitler.

"I want my ashes to lie on the banks of the Seine, amidst the French people I have so loved".

The bronze door.

Statue of Napoleon I, by Seurre, formerly standing on top of the column in Place Vendôme.

Eglise du Dôme: the high altar.

The Emperor's tomb.

Exterior of the Eglise du Dôme.

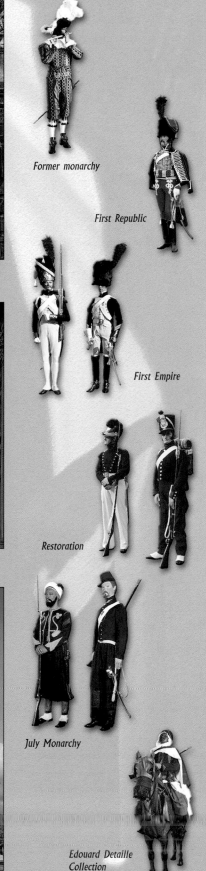

Former monarchy

First Republic

First Empire

Restoration

July Monarchy

Edouard Detaille Collection

MUSEE DE L'ARMEE

The Musée des Plans-Reliefs has on display a hundred or so models (1: 600) of fortresses and fortified villages of France.

Relief map of the palace of the kings of Mallorca in Perpignan made in 1701.

Relief map of Mont Saint-Michel made in 1701.

MONTPARNASSE TOWER

When the former Montparnasse station no longer met the needs of SNCF, it was knocked down and the Tour Montparnasse and its shopping centre built on the cleared site. The tower was built between 1969 and 1974. All of its 58 floors, including 54 floors of offices measuring nearly 2000 m2 each represents a superstructure of 112,000 m2, with a flat roof creating a 59th floor, open to the public. Architects: Beaudouin, Cassan, de Marien and Saubot. Height: 210 m - Weight: 120,000 tonnes - Lifts: 25 – Reinforced-concrete core: 70m deep foundations. Tour Montparnasse, one of the landmark buildings of the 20th century, stands at the centre of the capital. The top affords an extraordinary panorama on 2 floors open to the public: the 56th floor, roofed and air-conditioned, reached by the fastest lift in Europe (195 m in 38 seconds); the 59th floor, the highest and biggest roof terrace in Paris, the only point from which it is possible to view the capital through 360° and distances of up to 40 km.

ECOLE MILITAIRE
(former royal officers' training school)

Founded by edict of King Louis XV in 1751, it was intended to train 500 cadets of modest means. It was built between 1751 and 1773 by the architect Jacques-Ange Gabriel who revised his plans several times, aiming to outdo Les Invalides. After having been the summit of French horsemanship, from 1878 the building housed the military academy. In front of it, looking towards the Champ de Mars, stands the equestrian statue of Marshal Joffre, hero of the Great War.

EIFFEL TOWER

In 1884, under the Third Republic, the French government decided to hold a World Fair in 1889, for which it wished to have constructed a monument unlike anything ever seen before. Several projects arrived on the desk of the minister, Lockroy, including plans by Bourdais, architect of the Trocadéro, who proposed the construction of a "Sun Tower" one thousand feet high. Maurice Koechlin and Emile Nouguier, colleagues of Eiffel, with whom the architect Stephen Sauvestre was to be associated, had the idea of a metal tower some 300 m high. Interested in the project, Gustave Eiffel took it over and won the competition held by the government in 1886. Work began on 26 January 1887, despite the protests of many prominent people, including Guy de Maupassant, Charles Gounod, Victorien Sardou and others. The site employed hundreds of workers and it necessitated 700 drawings to make the 18,000 parts of the tower. These were assembled using 2,500,000 rivets and work progressed at an average 15 m per month. It was officially opened on 30 March 1889. The result was spectacularly light: despite weighing 10,000 tonnes, the tower only exerts the same pressure on the ground as a man seated in a chair (4 kg/cm^2)! Nevertheless, in order to reach the first floor at 57 m, 360 steps must be climbed, then 380 to reach the second at 155 m, and another 1062 to reach the top at a height of 300 m. Fortunately lifts were installed whose machinery is still functioning today. Built as part of the exhibition, the tower was to have been demolished at the end of the concession obtained by Eiffel, in 1909. It was saved by radiotelegraphy and its military applications, among others: the interception of coded messages during the Great War, which most notably led to the arrest of the spy Mata-Hari. Continuing its career on the airwaves, the tower was improved in 1957 with television equipment which took its height to 320.75 m.

Love goes like this running water
Love goes
Slow as life
And violent as Hope

Days pass and weeks pass
Neither time past
Nor love comes back
beneath Mirabeau bridge [where] flows the Seine

Come the night sound the hour
Days go by [yet] I remain

(Extract from a poem by Guillaume Apollinaire,
Mirabeau Bridge)

At the southern tip of Allée des Cygnes, the statue of "Liberty Lighting the World", a bronze miniature of Bartholdi's original.

Palais de Chaillot (architects: Boileau, Carlu and Azéma) built for the 1937 World Fair.

VERSAILLES

Motivated equally by his concern to distance himself from the bourgeois and the people of Paris, whose inclination to insurrection and riot had punctuated his childhood, and to keep the great nobles, indeed all the nobility, under his control, Louis XIV transformed Louis XIII's hunting lodge so that he could move his government there permanently, creating a magnificent royal walled town, a temple to absolute power, where ritualised etiquette ruled the life of the court of the world's most powerful monarch.

Entry to the château is via Place des Armes, enclosed by entrance gates surmounted with the royal coat of arms. After the forecourt with its large round paving stones, you enter the Cour des Ministres [Ministers' Courtyard], passing the equestrian statue of Louis XIV. You then reach the Cour de Marbre [Marble Courtyard], enclosed by Louis XIII's small château where the Sun King lived, in the apartments behind the three high windows of the balcony. The architects Le Vau, François d'Orbay and Jules Hardouin-Mansart extended the wings of the original building, giving it a new splendour.

From the gardens created by the landscape gardener Le Nôtre, the magnificence of the building can be fully appreciated. Before it, the Tapis Vert [Green Carpet] unfurls, with the waters of the Apollo Basin adding interest.

Portrait of Louis XIV, by Rigaud.

Grand Trianon, constructed in 1687 by Jules Hardouin-Mansart.

Galerie des Batailles [Gallery of Battles].

Galerie des Glaces [Hall of Mirrors].

The Queen's hamlet in the gardens of the Petit Trianon.

Parterres du Midi [southern section of the open terraces].

Below the Parterres du Midi are huge steps leading down to another masterpiece by Jules Hardouin-Mansart, the Orangerie. Taking advantage of its aspect, Le Nôtre planted a group of unusual trees on the steep slope. And the architect here constructed a glasshouse of absolutely classical simplicity and power.

The King's apartments. ▶

◀ *Temple de l'Amour [Temple of Love]*

Bassin de Latone. [Latona Basin] ▼

KING'S KITCHEN GARDEN

At the initiative of the Sun King, who wished to have excellent fruit and vegetables served at his table, Jean-Baptiste de la Quintinie created a garden between 1678 and 1683 to match the appetite of his sovereign. Laid out near the Pièce d'eau des Suisses, on the site of the "l'Etang puant" [stinking pond], it was designed to be "in a convenient location for the walks and the satisfaction of the King". Occupying an area of twenty-five arpents (about nine hectares), its layout has changed very little to this day: the Grand Carré, composed of sixteen vegetable patches or "carrés" arranged around a central pool, surrounded by twenty-nine orchards of fruit trees. A terrace overlooks the whole kitchen garden from where Louis XIV would have had a grandstand view of the crops and the endless dance of the forty or so gardeners employed at the time. To regale the royal palace, La Quintinie carried out trials with plants to improve the look of the produce and achieve early cropping. Adjusting exposure to the sun, using manure from the nearby stables, effectively treating any plant diseases that appeared, using covers and cloches to protect fragile plants, he obtained spectacular results, envied by the courts of Europe. On La Quintinie's death in 1688, several families of gardeners succeeded one another, and kept the tradition of using the Potager du Roi as a place of experimentation. The Le Normand family developed the cultivation of asparagus, introduced the first coffee bushes and built a Dutch greenhouse (1732) enabling Louis XV, three years later, to taste the first pineapple. The Potager du Roi became an experimental garden of the school of Versailles in 1798, under the iron rule of botanist Antoine Richard, appointed by the French National Convention. Between 1801 and 1815 a "National Nursery" was set up to select the best fruit varieties. More greenhouses were put up, enabling a banana tree to produce its first fruits in 1840.

Used by the National Agronomy Institute (1848) for applied horticulture, the kitchen garden became the National Horticulture School in 1874, with the addition, at the initiative of Auguste Hardy, of 1900 vegetable species and a rose garden with 800 varieties of roses. The school then gained an international reputation at the same time as moving into landscape art. This discipline became increasingly important and a decree of 1976 founded the Ecole Nationale Supérieure du Paysage (ENSP) concentrating on landscape gardening, while the Ecole Nationale Supérieure d'Horticulture (ENSH) left Versailles for Angers.

Alongside the Potager, the Parc Balbi (currently being restored), designed by the architect Chalgrin (1785) on the Anglo-Chinese model, allowed the Comte de Provence to enjoy the country air, sheltered by a pavilion which was demolished following the Revolution. The site, like the Potager du Roi, has been classified a historic monument since 1926.

STADE DE FRANCE®

In 1988, France ran as a candidate to host the last Football World Cup of the 20th century in 1998. To qualify it had to equip itself with a large stadium seating at least 60,000 people. The Saint-Denis site was finally chosen for this new Parisian temple to sport.

The Stade de France® is today the biggest modular stadium in the world and the biggest open-air theatre in France. Designed by four French architects, Macary, Zubléna, Regembal and Costantini, it has 80,000 seats under cover. It is a multipurpose events venue, which hosts the biggest sporting events (6 Nations Tournament, the matches of the France football and rugby teams...), mega-concerts and varied shows.

Put up in record time (31 months), the Stade de France® has a number of remarkable architectural features including a suspended elliptical roof of an area equivalent to the Place de la Concorde and a mobile grandstand seating 25,000 which can be moved back 15 m to uncover the full athletics track.

Open to the general public since 1998, this exceptional building is open every day to visitors wishing to discover its secrets.

Stade
de
France®

DISNEYLAND® RESORT PARIS

Located in Marne-la-Vallée, 32 km east of Paris, DISNEYLAND® RESORT PARIS has become a must for tourists visiting the capital. Young and old will find that this magical world created by Walt Disney in an enchanted setting with rides and attractions, has something for everyone. A range of refreshment stalls and restaurants ensure visitor comfort, and for those lucky enough to be staying longer, hotels offer themed accommodation with staff in costume. An array of shops ensures that everyone can take home a souvenir of their journey to the kingdom of the imagination.

Covering an area of 57 hectares, the park is divided into 5 "lands" each with rides, attractions, food outlets and shops on a particular theme:

- **"MAIN STREET, U.S.A."**, creates the atmosphere of small-town America at the turn of the century.

- **"FRONTIERLAND"**, a real boom town of the West during the gold rush era.

- **"ADVENTURELAND"**, Africa, the Caribbean, the jungle - the meeting place for all explorers.

- **"FANTASYLAND"**, the world of make-believe and fairy tales which you enter through *le Château de la Belle au Bois Dormant*.

- **"DISCOVERYLAND"**, the future world in a setting which Jules Verne might have created.

Located between the theme park and the hotels, near the RER / TGV station, Disney® Village recreates a typically American atmosphere with bars, shops, discos and restaurants; Dinner and Show at *"La Légende de Buffalo Bill"*.

Le Château de La Belle au Bois Dormant in Fantasyland.

Indiana Jones™ et le Temple du Péril... à l'envers! in Adventureland.

Captain Hook's Galley in Adventureland.

Le Château de La Belle au Bois Dormant in Fantasyland.

Big Thunder Mountain in Frontierland.

Orbitron, Space Mountain in Discoveryland.

PARC WALT DISNEY STUDIOS©
"Behind the scenes" at the cinema

Opened in 2002, this new theme park adjoins the DISNEY-LAND® RESORT PARIS park and offers visitors a full day of family fun. You will also find shops and restaurants on a

FRONTLOT Disney Studio 1.

tour offering plenty of activities.

The site is divided into four "production zones" which reveals what goes on behind the camera at each one: sets, rigging, animation, special effects, costumes...

-**"FRONT LOT"**: a Hollywood set on a boulevard of dreams at Disney Studio 1.

-**"ANIMATION COURTYARD"**: the art of Disney-style animation or inspired by the manipulation technique originating in Japan with *Animagique*® or based on animated drawing as in *Les Tapis Volants*.

-**"PRODUCTION COURTYARD"**: *CinéMagique* transports the spectator right inside a film, *Television Production Tour* reveals what goes on behind the scenes of Disney Chanel France, while *Studio Tram Tour*® illustrates in a very realistic way the art of set design and special effects, notably at *Catastrophe Canyon*®.

-**"BACKLOT"**: special effects with *Armageddon*, the speed and music of *Rock'n Roller Coaster avec Aerosmith*, the blockbuster stunts of *Moteurs... Action! Spectacle de Cascades*.

Between two attractions, improvising actors - the Streetmospheres – interact with the visitor and let him play the actor in turn in humorous sketches or "real mock filming", thus fulfilling Walt Disney's vow for: "each family to find themselves plunged in a succession of extraordinary adventures and live shows".

BACKLOT: Moteurs... Action! Spectacle de Cascades.

PRODUCTION COURTYARD:
Studio Tram Tour® Catastrophe Canyon®.

BACKLOT: Moteurs... Action! Spectacle de Cascades.

NOW IN PRODUCTION:
Tapis Volant
FLYING CARPETS OVER AGRAB AH

ANIMATION
COURTYARD:
Les Tapis Volants.

PRODUCTION COURTYARD: CinéMagique

BACKLOT: Moteurs... Action! Spectacle de Cascades.